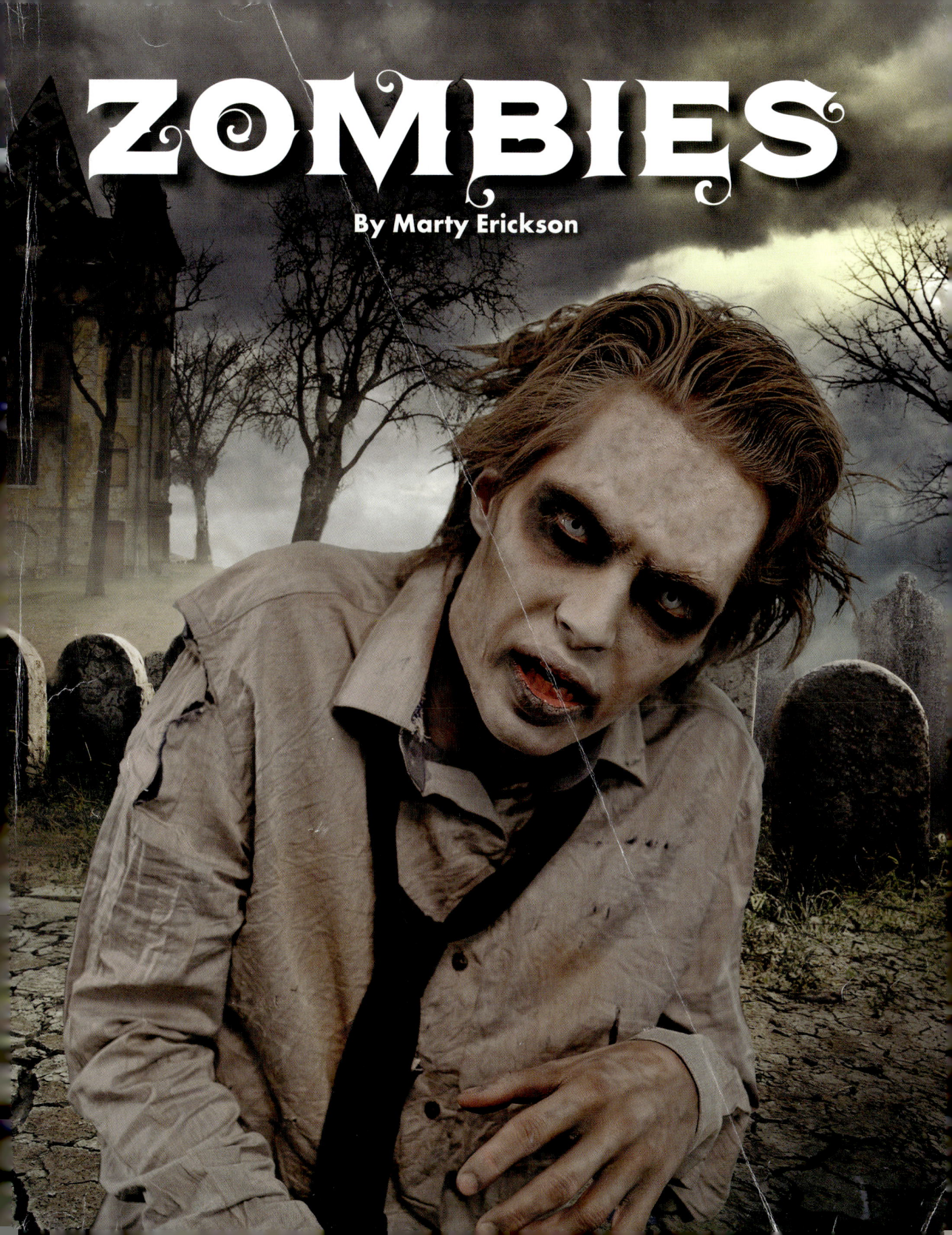

Published by The Child's World®
1980 Lookout Drive • Mankato, MN 56003-1705
800-599-READ • www.childsworld.com

Photographs ©: Shutterstock Images, cover (zombie), cover (background), 1 (zombie), 1–3 (background), 12–13, 16, 17, 23; Market Square Productions/Album/Newscom, 5; Joe Prachatree/Shutterstock Images, 6; Lukiyanova Natalia Frenta/Shutterstock Images, 7, 24; Red Line Editorial, 9; United Artists/Album/Newscom, 11; Leo Lin Tang/Shutterstock Images, 15; D. Kucharski K. Kucharska/Shutterstock Images, 19; Ash T. Productions/Shutterstock Images, 20; Lenscap Photography/Shutterstock Images, 21

Copyright © 2022 by The Child's World®
All rights reserved. No part of this book may be reproduced or utilized in any form or by any means without written permission from the publisher.

ISBN 9781503850293 (Reinforced Library Binding)
ISBN 9781503850866 (Portable Document Format)
ISBN 9781503851627 (Online Multi-user eBook)
LCCN 2021939645

Printed in the United States of America

Table of Contents

CHAPTER ONE

It's Alive!...4

CHAPTER TWO

History of Zombies...8

CHAPTER THREE

Dead or Ill?...14

CHAPTER FOUR

Zombies Today...18

Glossary...22

To Learn More...23

Index...24

CHAPTER ONE
IT'S ALIVE!

Suki and her mom sat on the couch. Every Friday they watched a new horror movie. Tonight, they picked out *Night of the Living Dead*. Suki's mom said it was the best zombie movie. They turned off the lights and snacked on popcorn. The black-and-white film played on the TV screen.

Suki clutched at her blanket. A zombie lumbered through a graveyard. His suit was torn and dirty. He followed a woman. The woman ran to her car. She locked the doors. But she did not have her keys.

Night of the Living Dead *is the inspiration for many modern zombie movies.*

The zombie tried to get into the car. He took a rock and broke the window. The woman released the emergency brake. The car began to roll down a hill. The zombie was not able to keep up.

Zombies are undead creatures that feed on living people.

Zombies are legendary creatures. They are human in form. But they do not act like people. Zombies have been changed by magic or disease. Stories of zombies became common in Haiti. Then they spread around the world. Over time, stories about zombies changed. But one thing has stayed the same. Zombie stories continue to hold people's imaginations.

In many stories, zombies rise from the grave.

CHAPTER TWO
HISTORY OF ZOMBIES

Belief in zombies goes back hundreds of years. Beginning in the 1500s, Europeans kidnapped people from West Africa. The Europeans forced these people to go to the Americas. The Europeans enslaved them. Some enslaved people were taken to Haiti. Haiti is an island in the Caribbean.

West African peoples held on to their **cultural** and religious beliefs. A *zombi* was a god in some West African communities. Over time, Haitians developed their own unique culture.

Haitian Vodou, or voodoo, is a type of religion. Vodou continues the belief in *zombi*. In Vodou, a *zombi* is a person brought back from the dead. The *zombi* is forced to follow the orders of the person who raised it from the dead.

In the early 1900s, white Americans and Europeans who visited Haiti were inspired by the *zombi* stories. They made books and films influenced by Haitian beliefs.

Many of these early stories stayed close to the religious practices of Vodou. Zombie stories focused on a sorcerer. The undead person was forced to obey the sorcerer. Over time, stories about zombies began to change.

White Zombie is an early zombie movie. Actor Bela Lugosi plays a sorcerer who turns a woman into a zombie.

Some zombie stories are not really about the zombies. They are focused on the humans trying to survive.

Zombies that most people think of today were inspired by the 1968 film *Night of the Living Dead*. These zombies were people that came back from the dead. They fed on people. However, the word *zombie* was never used in the film.

The filmmaker was not inspired directly by Vodou. He called the creatures ghouls. Fans began to call them zombies. The name stuck. The director continued to make zombie films.

CHAPTER THREE

DEAD OR ILL?

Some stories of zombies say they were raised from the dead. Others say zombies are caused by a **virus** or **radiation** that affects the brain. The virus causes the person's brain to change. Zombies may become violent. Or they may have a big appetite. Many **characteristics** of zombies are similar from one story to the next.

Zombies often move slowly. But some stories have running zombies. Few things can stop a zombie. A zombie's brain is different from a person's. Stories say zombies do not feel pain. Injuries usually do not stop a zombie.

In many zombie stories, humans have to work hard to fight off zombies.

Zombies never seem to feel full. Stories of zombies often say they eat people. Zombies do not have free will. They are focused only on eating.

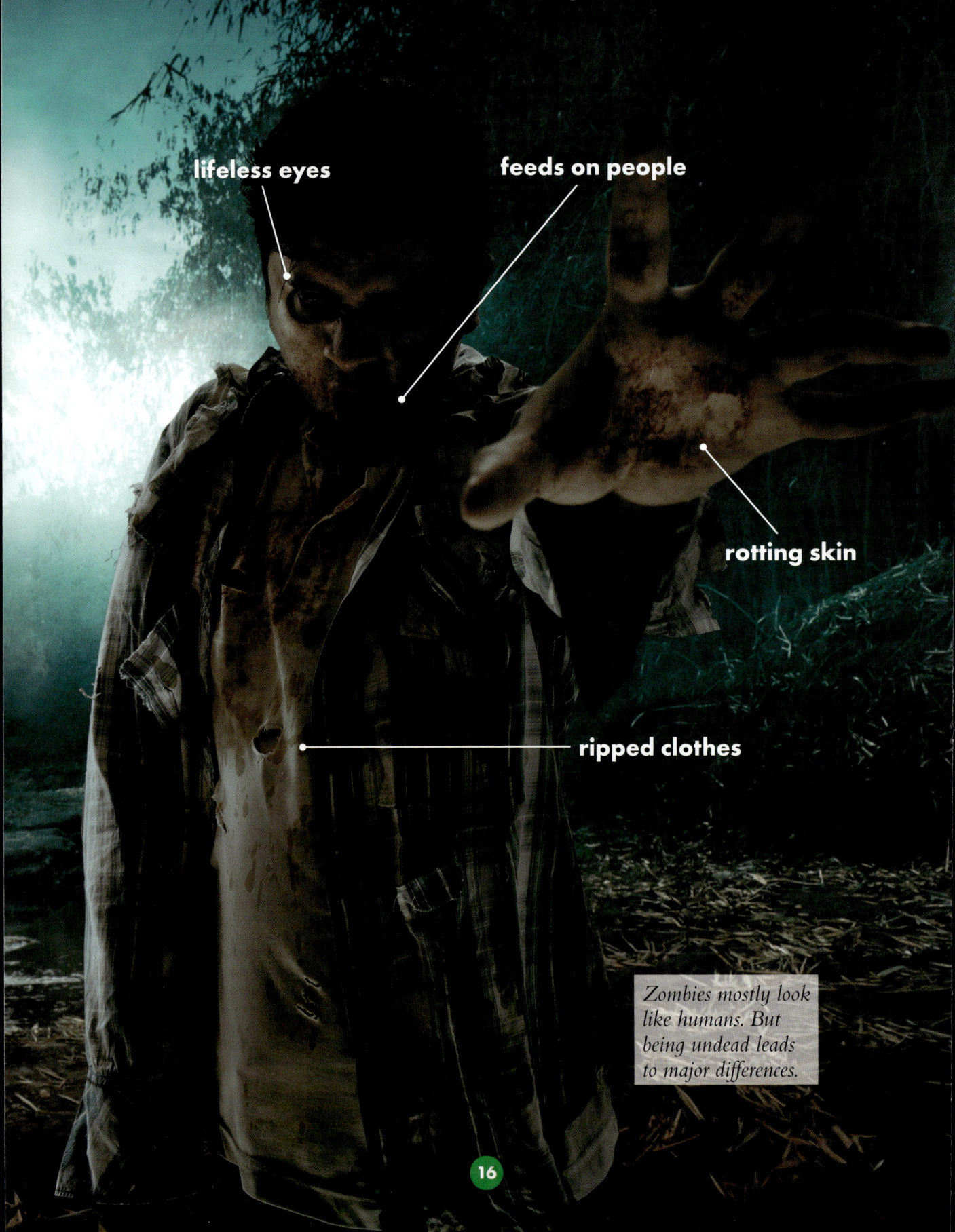

Zombies mostly look like humans. But being undead leads to major differences.

Zombies look like people. But being undead gives them a unique appearance. Many zombies have sunken eyes and shrunken lips. This happens as their bodies begin to rot. Zombies may also have injuries from when they died. Their clothes may be ripped.

In some stories, zombies can be cured. But many stories say there is no way to cure a zombie. Most of these stories say the only way to stop a zombie is to destroy its brain.

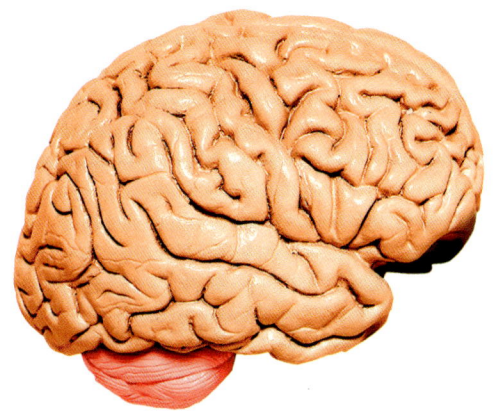

CHAPTER FOUR
ZOMBIES TODAY

Human zombies do not exist. But zombielike creatures do exist in the animal kingdom. One kind of **parasite** lays its eggs in snails. The parasite takes over the snail's eyestalks. It causes them to become brightly colored. The snail cannot hide from birds. A bird eats the snail. Then the parasite infects the bird.

Another example of a zombielike parasite is a type of wasp. This wasp lays eggs in a caterpillar. The eggs use the caterpillar for food and protection until they hatch. The caterpillar dies when the young wasps hatch. Like zombies, the caterpillars and snails are taken over by an outside force.

A zombielike worm has infected this snail's eyestalk. The infected eyestalk is green and striped. The bright colors make birds more likely to eat the snail.

People continue to be fascinated by the idea of zombies. Some scientists even study what it would take for a zombie **apocalypse** to happen. They study diseases and other infections. So far, scientists believe it is unlikely zombies will ever exist.

Scientists study diseases to help prevent outbreaks.

Minecraft is a popular video game. Players sometimes have to fight zombies.

Zombies inspire books, TV shows, video games, and movies. For example, zombies are in the video game *Minecraft*. At some schools, students play Humans vs. Zombies. It is a school-wide game of tag. Some people are zombies. They tag and "infect" other students. Zombies are not real. But people continue to enjoy hearing and creating stories about zombies.

GLOSSARY

apocalypse (uh-POK-uh-lips) The apocalypse is the end of the world. Some stories feature a zombie apocalypse.

characteristics (kayr-uk-tur-ISS-tiks) Characteristics are things about a person, such as appearance or actions. Zombies have similar characteristics in many different stories.

cultural (KUL-chuhr-uhl) Cultural means having to do with a community's beliefs and traditions. People from West Africa continued their cultural practices in Haiti.

parasite (PAYR-uh-syt) A parasite is an animal that takes over the body of another animal. One parasite can cause a snail's eyestalks to become brightly colored.

radiation (ray-dee-AY-shun) Radiation is harmful energy. Some stories about zombies say the creatures are created through radiation.

virus (VY-rus) A virus is a microscopic organism or protein that causes disease, such as the flu. In some stories, a virus causes humans to become zombies.

TO LEARN MORE

In the Library

Klepeis, Alicia Z. *Haiti*. Minneapolis, MN: Bellwether Media, 2020.

Nagle, Frances. *Zombies*. New York, NY: Gareth Stevens Publishing, 2017.

Stiefel, Chana. *Animal Zombies!* Washington, DC: National Geographic, 2018.

On the Web

Visit our website for links about zombies:

childsworld.com/links

Note to Parents, Teachers, and Librarians: We routinely verify our Web links to make sure they are safe and active sites. So encourage your readers to check them out!

INDEX

appearance, 4, 17

behavior, 4–5, 9–10, 12, 14–15

disease, 7, 14, 20

games, 21

Haiti, 7, 8–10

magic, 7, 9–10

Night of the Living Dead, 4–5, 12–13

parasites, 18

science, 20
slavery, 8

Vodou, 9–10, 13

ABOUT THE AUTHOR

Marty Erickson is a writer living in Minnesota. They write books for young people full time and like to go hiking.